Having Decided To Stay

Bryana Joy Johnson

Printed in the United States of America

First Printing, 2012

ISBN-13: 978-0615680699
ISBN-10: 0615680690

Ethandune Publishing
P.O. Box 79
Royce City, Texas 75189
www.ethandunepublishing.com
info@ethandunepublishing.com

DEDICATED
with much love to

Meryem 'Rosemary'
who gave me a reason to find the language
of song delightful and worth studying

and

Hannah Rebecca Keeler, whose jubilance has
infected me and whose words have been
sunk deep into my life

ACKNOWLEDGEMENTS

for my Mom, who presented me with the words of the lyricists and the bards and allowed me to simply drink them in,

for my Dad, who introduced me to the world's most epic poem : *The Ballad of the White Horse* ,

for Shannon, who has shared my appreciation for the master wordsmiths and my disgust with the pretenders,

for the Utmost Christian Writers' Foundation and the Homeschool Legal Defense Association for the opportunities and incentive they provided me to discover the music inside and offer it to the world,

for Emily Dickinson, who taught me to rely heavily on those charming little dashes —

for Tennyson who gave us *Enoch Arden* and *Crossing the Bar* and *"men may come and men may go, but I go on forever,"*

for Ann Voskamp, whose dedication to celebration was utilized by very God to convince me to stay in the first place,

grateful thanksgiving from knees here and

soli deo gloria

TABLE OF CONTENTS

Having Decided to Stay   13

After Psalm 23   14

About-Face   15

Found   16

The Hound of Heaven   17

The Quintessence of Dust   19

The Saying It   21

That You Love One Another   22

Fairy-Tale   24

The Grudge   25

Resurrection   29

Sharbat Gula   30

The Last Sleeping Moment   32

Gate-Greeter   34

David   35

Cantata #147 Summer   37

Dead Men Walking   39

Enoch Arden   41

We Do Believe in Miracles   42

Beatrix   43

Nevertheless Come Autumn   44

Delirium   45

For A Boy Child   47

Katczinsky   48
Never Never Land   49
The Importance of Being Earnest   50
When This is Over   51
Saint Crispin's Day   52
Wax And All   54
Enfeebling   56
The Shadow of the Ransoming Wood   57
The Knowing Tree   58
Superlative   59
Jonah   61
Confession   62
Apologetics   63
Hallelujah Chorus   64
Christmas is a House   65
The Image   66
Residence   67

"I would maintain that thanks
are the highest form of thought,
and that gratitude is happiness
doubled by wonder."

[G.K. Chesterton]

HAVING DECIDED TO STAY

I have erected my castle amidst graffiti, dead grass,
and potholes, chipped bricks and mutilated cats.
I intend to sojourn a very long time, put out
roots, hang flags and flowerboxes, tame roses.
I shall make an end of taking to the clouds,
fragmenting, and airlines and leaving things behind,
of German on sky radio, and the sad sound
of engines multiplying the miles in between.

I intend to make them my people who people
this unwhole place, to be of them, to be an
outsider no longer, to no longer stand aloof.
No Pygmalion spent more time chiseling on knees
than I intend to do. I intend to embrace the soil
of this place, to clear the air with true stories and a
wholesale slaughter of lies; to garden so immaculately
that everyone will talk about our roses.

I intend to love you here also
as I have loved you in every other place.

AFTER PSALM 23

In the presence of mine enemies,
in the presence of mine goggle-eyed doubts,
mine palpitating, white-knuckled *no*'s,
by the light of the fuse,
by the shimmer of deadly fireworks,
the glint, the glare, the grenades,
in the grey shadow of death,
in the serpentine breath
where mine snakes circle tight,
tangled, flapping forks,
in the mud of mine trenches,
by the bullet that wrenches
flesh from skin in the dark,
in the shade of my looming nightmare
of the minefields and the blade
is my lover's table laid.
We are so jubilant we spill red wine
over everything – trembly-fingered,
splash it on the tablecloth, the bread,
and watch the cracks soak red.

(First published in the Fall 2011/Spring 2012 issue of *Assisi Journal*)

ABOUT-FACE

If you unzip
the morning of departure
misty-eyed and

your fingers fumble,
falter with your falling face,
and home seems

suddenly sacred and
seductive in the colors
of dawn – clean,

the coffee redolent
of love and the clink
of cups precious

like a last kiss in
wartime, well
maybe you should stay.

(First published in *Adroit Journal*)

FOUND

I scratch down happiness, I
want my ink to do happy dances,
to careen across the pages staggering
like a drunken fellow, giddy
on moonshine or sunset.

Not because in all this cacophony
of locusts I want to be FDR's
foolish optimist, desperate
to deny the dark, refusing to
reel, to shudder, until the last
clutching hangnail snaps.

But only because I really am
found. And I will not shut up. I
will express it with booming
enthusiasm from the house-tips. I
am all about talking about it.

THE HOUND OF HEAVEN

He put a hound on you – I asked Him to –
an animal with gasping, wild breath,
and groping teeth and lunging, starving eyes,
and he will catch you: it's as sure as death.

Two miles from town and by the clock of night
1:00 in the morning, we found prints of yours
tracking the snow with frightened sneaker-feet
and followed them right to the bolted door.

By windowlight I saw your silhouette,
made out your shape, your blackness, in that room.
"Snap leashes! Subject bolting for the door!"
and all His dogs came raging after you.

We watch you jerk through darkness from the steps,
and hurtle over winterfallen white
and after you they come like bullet bursts
and howls curdle blood and chill the night.

Your sleeping days are over – you will run,
your sitting-down time gone – you will pound feet.
We love you and the only way to show
it, is to free you from your sultry peace.

The world rolled out before you – you have room
Press hard heels into firm dirt – you can run,
You have a lifetime to attempt escape:
go for it – let us know when you are done.

You will not tear forever over fields,

and up the rocks and crannies of the walls –
you will not run the circle of the world
unending – someday you will trip and fall.

You will wear tired and you will miss steps –
someday toes slide and you will feel the ledge.
His hounds will find your flesh and meet their teeth
through frenzied skin, and drag you from the edge.

I told Him softly, "I have one I love,
one distant and one orphaned from the day.
Maybe you could send a couple dogs
To take him down and bring him in someday?"

(*The Hound of Heaven* was awarded an honorable mention
in 2010 Utmost Christian Writers Novice Contest
and was originally published as part of that contest.)

THE QUINTESSENCE OF DUST
(*in war-time*)

Under this majestic roof fretted with golden fire,
what a piece of work is every one of us,
lank and lacerated in the last sunset ever,
gaunt in the glare of the final pink light.
It will be good to go down with you, my brothers,
for the acrid smolder curling out of Wielun and
for our dead horses row on row; Guernica,
and the steam rising off of the rubble-choked Thames.
It will be good to go down with you
in the war for the soul of the world.

Put your hot hands out for the wind and
lean into the rippling of the green, the oscillation
of the happy fields where the leaves of pearly corn
are gilded with days-end. And thank God for
the foliage and the wet and the blue that is.
If this grasping flood of flame should overtake us,
lick the globe up with madly dancing tongues,
spatter our cinders on the moon – thank God for the
spring-fresh acid of red strawberries, the yellow silk
of furled ribbons, and the nightingales that were.

From the wrinkle-red squalling, first drawing in
to lungs, what a piece of craft and curvature
have our breaths been! What a piece of work is every
man of us, two-legged and tender, brute-strong and brave,
like shy Quasimodos encompassed by confusion.
If I fall on the arid upper-crust,
crumple under fireballs, felled by the flaring guns,

break my parts in pieces, bleed out,
it is something to have gazed on the constellated white,
felt it running from the eyes and the pores: the salt of love.

It is something to have whispered wild *thank-yous*
in the only ways we know how.

(*The Quintessence of Dust in Wartime* won 2nd place
in the 2012 Utmost Christian Writers Contest
and was originally published as part of that contest.)

THE SAYING IT

The saying it,
maybe stuttered, scared,
cold with shaking teeth,
maybe anxious breathed,

the spitting out,
maybe fast distracted,
incoherent, quick;
maybe just half,
– but just yours –
spins the world.

(First published in *Time Of Singing Literary Magazine*)

THAT YOU LOVE ONE ANOTHER

In the beginning was the Word, and the Word was with God,
and the Word was God…and the light shines into the darkness
and the darkness has not overcome it. —The Gospel of John, Chapter 1

that your joy may be full, every
    buttercup glossy, and the lichen
        green crawling up the steep and the
            mossy banks of the algae-blue pond,
                too immaculate with bubbles and
                    bryophyte fronds for explaining.
That your pores secrete sheer love
    here – residue of living – and your
        tongue flap, always giving names to
            the sweetness of the way. Slap
                the globe under a crystal coverslip,
                    and tip the slide to rays and after all
                      you can go ahead and call it good.
That the blueberries dotted
    juice-busting in the pancakes be
        perfect and the hurts and the
            headaches treated with the best
                medicine – joy *incandescent*, Edison,
                  that glows outward and around
                    into light and surround sound.
That sirens clang music on the
    inside drums. And after, when the
        crying comes, that *you remember Me.*
            Oh, that you not forget! That you by
                no means waste the wine-red cup,
                  that you break flesh into breadcrumbs

and taste the ways I poured it into you.
Friends, I have called you friends
and given you the oceanic unplumbed
places, scratched your faces with
unsounded depths and sight
that you might know the breadth,
the width, the height so well you speak
it in your sleep, murmur it to the
cold, the blaze alike, let it take hold.
That you not forget in all the flood, the
flailing, about the blood, the nailing
flesh on wood while the pulse roars,
the life ebbs out for them – the
friends, you know. In the end, on the
bend around the road where the rubber
meets the asphalt and the mud-splash
splatters and things count,
well this will be all that matters.

(*That Your Joy May Be Full* won 1st place in the 2011 Utmost Christian Writers Contest and was originally published as part of that contest.)

FAIRY-TALE

Suppose they really did live happily ever after.
Suppose Cinderella was a good wife – and she
could have been. I daresay she was reticent,
timid, not one to make a fuss, or rock the boat,
accustomed to orders and quiet in company.
Suppose he was a good husband, the haughty
prince, coddled from the cradle up. He might have
pulled it off. He was in love after all, and love
covers a multitude of offenses. Perhaps it
wrapped up her social poverty and rough edges
and lack of table manners in velvet
and smoothed everything and the
royal lovebirds got along just fine after all.
Suppose that Belle forgot the beast-horns, the
stamped image of his face framed with fur.
Suppose she one day wrapped around his
neck and felt only man-flesh there. Suppose
Snow White stopped having nightmares about
old women peddling apples, hook-nosed, cloaked,
warted and long-fingered on her doorstep in the dusk.
Suppose her prince one day learned to sleep the
nights through, his fingers in her hair, no fear of
jerking eyes wide to her screaming.
I retain my right to believe in happy endings.

(A slightly differnt version was first published in the
2011 Winter issue of the *Boston Literary Magazine*.)

THE GRUDGE

We had a thunder in the night that came
like evil laughter heralding the rain.
I woke and found my city half-asleep,
and I put on old shoes to walk the street.
We have too many cars here on my block,
even in blinding rain at three'o'clock.
I know I'm not the first one to complain –
don't we all hate our cities just the same?

I turned to take a back-alley and found
God, sitting in a puddle on the ground.
It'd been awhile since we'd kept in touch
but I could see He hadn't changed that much.
"Where have you been?" I asked Him kinda slow,
"I'm pretty sure the whole world wants to know
if God has sent us coasting down a hill,
and took off work and left the steering wheel."

I hoped to see a fire light His face,
to kneel there conquered by a flaming grace.
God didn't look up from *The New York Times*,
"Go on," He said, "what else is on your mind?"
The sullen anger seething in my head
exploded into wild wrath instead.
"I have a list, get ready!" I half yelled.
"When I'm done, see if you can do as well!

I want to know why you hate innocents,
and why you feed the world at their expense.
I want to know why God has set apart,
and holds a grudge against the pure in heart.

If God is sovereign, He cannot be just,
(And I'm prepared to prove it if I must).
If God is just, He has no final say –
Judge of the Earth, you need a Judgment Day.

We had a knifing right here yesterday –
a good man going on his quiet way.
I want to hear you say you did not see:
it will make it much easier for me.
We have a lot of babies, clean, unborn,
unstained, and quite unwanted and so torn
with scissors in a sanitary space.
Tell me you have not seen this taking place.

What of the kids that line our night-time streets,
and sell themselves because they have to eat?
I know you passed a few outside that store –
God, don't you help the children anymore?
When one who loves you lets his whole world go,
why doesn't God who saved Abednego
take His scared, trusting lover from the flame,
and bring a matchless glory to His name?

Three times beaten with rods and one time stoned,
Thrice shipwrecked, one night in the deep alone.'
Is this the way God sees the blessed meek?
As targets for death and calamity?
The Devil roams the streets and countryside
and takes whom he shall find and rips him wide.
The wretched righteous call you through the years –
please tell me you have cotton in your ears!

God set the evening news down in the mud,
and smiled, like I dared to hope He would.

And in that one igniting of His eyes,
was life and death and sunset and sunrise.
All shades of stars within the Milky Way,
and all the flaming colors of the day,
the passion of the surf upon the sand,
and laughing of the ship in sight of land,

the holy joy of altar-kneeling tears,
through all the multitude of counted years,
the sparkle of a thousand glories dead,
hung, hovered in his smile when He said,
"You say the 'pure in heart' – I've known one man
and only one since all the world began.
All outrages, all wounds to soul and skin,
pale when compared with what was done to Him.

Those hands bound, that cheek slapped upon the kiss,
that head crowned thorny – yes, I lived through *this*.
Those shoulders robed in mockery and shame,
and all the hurting spitting out the Name.
That back bared, those arms stretched to take the sting!
A man can look at almost anything,
but this wrong wrongs the one that has to watch:
the eye can take a lot, but not that much.

Go on and tell Me what I should have done
– all forces of the universe My own –
Tell Me I should have held the striking hand,
and sent that legion scouring the land.
You will be right. My child, you will be right.
But tell Me what you would have done that night:
would you have spared the blood within that heart?
And left the children crying in the dark?"

I thought that I had other things to say –
The wind picked up and took my breath away.

(*The Grudge* won 2nd place in the Homeschool Legal Defense
Association's 2010 Poetry Contest and was originally published
as part of that contest.)

RESURRECTION

If the resurrection really happened
like we say it did,
if the kettle got to boiling and
popped the trembling lid,

if the blue shells in the garden that the
rain dumped down to wash
were the casings of the carcasses that
branched into the squash,

if the worm rolled back in horror from the
palpitating heart,
and a shudder set to scurrying
the beetles in the dark,

if the serpent with the smashed-in skull
has not recovered since:
I'm thinking that that ought to make
some kind of difference.

(Dedicated to Ann Voskamp,
who said that if the resurrection
is real, it should make a real difference.

First published in *Time Of Singing Literary Magazine*)

SHARBAT GULA (a portrait)

Girl, cold-countenanced,
    scared, with wild eyes –
        incandescent globes of green
            stretched in surprise.
Girl, skin red and real –
    sweat and shadows sit
        in the canyons of the face,
            making marks on it.
Girl, with the scarred nose,
    the red-scarf frame
        draped around the portrait
            that we give no name.
Girl, snagged on a flash,
    dirt around the mouth –
        dust of a war-racked
            country in the south.
Girl, dug out of a
    recordless land –
        no date of birth, no
            writ of her hand.
Girl, pulled tight by days,
    slipping down the veil
        off of dead youth and the
            hard and the pale.
Girl, you have grown a
    time-twisted face!
        I found a child in a
            refugee place –
I swear I did my best by her:
    set her up and took a fast picture.

Girl, half-covered head,
*   hair allowed to show --*
*   snapshot of a child dead*
*   A long time ago.*

(Her photograph, taken by Steve McCurry in 1984 at the Nasir Bagh refugee camp, has been named "*the most recognized photograph*" in the history of National Geographic magazine. But when the picture appeared on the June 1985 cover of National Geographic, her identity was a mystery. It was to remain so for 17 years, until, in January 2002, a National Geographic team traveled to Afghanistan to find the now-famous "Afghan Girl" and finally located Sharbat Gula, then around the age of 30, in a remote region of the county.)

THE LAST SLEEPING MOMENT

It's good of you to be here, to sit by the window
and hold your eyes open. Mine that are cloudy
cannot tell who you are – but it was good of you to come
sit awhile, watch a man dying.
The night has been a long time going by –
a long time for a fretful old man to fidget between the
blankets. But now that I know I will not see the morning,
one night maybe isn't such a long time after all.

Suddenly I want to say some last words, something
you could write down and be proud to have heard.
You'd say "I was there when the old man died. He said –"
if you weren't nodding a head too heavy, too long watching,
if you weren't snoring, dreaming on the windowpane.
"Last words are for fools who haven't said enough already."
Well, Marx, old man, you said more than enough. But me –
have I ever said anything worth saying in my whole life?

I feel my eyelids slipping –
not the withered, fleshy ones against the wet lens,
but the ones under, up against the Being, cutting off
the shapes of this dingy room and the candle flickering on
the wall. I also can't hear the quiet anymore. No
soundlessness of the death-watch and the middle of the
night. Instead, there is this splashing on rocks, so close I can
feel that the mist of the waterfall is cold, but still blurred in
with the fading dark.

I have been a long time dreaming but this is not like
the world blacking out, but like the glass darkly
is getting thinner, the veil keeping me in dreams falling off.

The stuff of Afterwards doesn't bubble into the picture
through a screen of boiling water so as to make you not-sure
it's real – like in the movies. Oh, there is water –
only water you can touch and splash fingers in
and slurp cold over the dry tongue.

I cannot see you anymore – you by the window –
the realness of this waterfall has closed in over you.
But I know you could still hear me if you weren't so fast
asleep, because right in the middle of the plunging white
still flutters that pathetic candle that called itself a light.
God, if he could see *this* light dumping over the mountains
like a million suns, feel this sharp infusion of aliveness!
Man, you would never, never sleep again.

Funny, I am not looking for them –
for the girl with the finger that wears my band of gold,
for the woman with the smile that the cancer took away
while a little boy watched it, begged her not to go.
The little boy is not looking for his two buried babies.
Instead I am wondering what exactly is a man with no last
words worth saying supposed to say to a very busy Judge
trying him for murder. And I'm guessing nothing.

You by the window,
giving in to the clock and the still night –
when you pass from that dream you're in to the next one,
find my clumsy heart still beneath the sheets, *thank you*.
It was good of you to sit awhile, watch a man waking up,
eyelids slipping right wide open.

(*The Last Sleeping Moment* was awarded an honorable mention in the 2011
Utmost Christian Writers Contest and was originally published as part of
that contest.)

GATE-GREETER

(September 18th, 2010 – in memory of Tim Wright)

You got there early? Not fair!
but all the better : when we come
by martyred twos and threes, worldworn,
or single ones, new children, young-adopted,
shell-shocked, not sure,
all us tired, barefoot staggering –
we'll know one gate-greeter for sure.
Peter maybe I won't know
– by sight, not at first –
but you, even decked in glory,
we will.

DAVID

I grow me a king in the scorch of the sun,
I grow him alone in the sand.
I give him – a child – the jackals of night.
I make him to master the land.

Out in the whistling wilderness wind,
I grow me a grace-deafened king –
the boy's ears are blocked to the whine of the world,
by the songs that the bulbul bird sings.

Down under the wide roof of twinkling light,
I grow me a wonder-awed king –
he knows to suck in long the smell of the night,
and dance in the dump of the rain.

I grow me a humbleheart king in the dirt,
a lowly and lovable lord,
a blister-kneed, clear-headed, clean-handed prince,
and this man I trust with a sword.

I send him a bloody-fanged lion who creeps
cat-quiet and soft in his stalk –
The child-king grapples, grows strong in his fear,
and strong in his love for the flock.

Soon now, little boy, who strangled the bear,
who snapped the gold neck of the cat,
you will face a man-monster for love of my lambs –
My king is made ready for that.

Come, child, sheepkeeper, and nursemaid of lambs,

song-wringer, proclaimer of glory –
the heart you are after has pulsed in your hands,
and this is the start of the story.

(*David* won 1st place in the Homeschool Legal Defense Association's
2011 Poetry Contest and was originally published as part of that contest.)

CANTATA #147 SUMMER

"Domino Possessori hisce notulis commendare se volebat J. S. Bach"

I send you a postcard of here –
      my daytimes and hardships
mingled with chlorine blue and
sweaty scraped sunscreen and
      the Little Boy's infectious childhood,
vibrant with eyes wide to good things.

We water a baby orchard,
      pave the cracked dirt with pond droplets,
bake out in the unrelenting blaze
with our sun-battered blackberries,
      wait together for mercy water from the sky.
And this is the good life.

I send you a writ of now,
      but I want it to be music –
notes like Bach's in curls and curves, wildly happy,
up-and-down, up-and-down melody of soaring,
      high to uncreated light.
Dying 'round the throne.

We slice peaches,
      fuzzy-skinned and splitting into juice,
fruit-ripeness alive in the kitchen,
tantalizing – the tongue must feel it –
      pack away gritty green pears
for after-autumn days and longer nights.

Be assured of storms –

that I will write to tell of rain,
be assured of frost flurries and Christmas trees,
frozen fingers and firelight, us tasting the gone-by
        summer in peaches and pears under cream,
#147 undermoon in mittens,

        soli-deo-gloria like always.

DEAD MEN WALKING

[For Peter and John]

And we were dead,
stark in our trespasses,
your unseeing eyes wide,
– mine too –
the smell of the grave on our lips.
It is the way of things,
the coursing of the world:
death begat death begat death begat death

We went racing,
our hearts and our toes
thudding in time together,
– I beat you.
She said there was nothing,
and I found the nothing first.
There was nothing.
You and me, how could we understand that?

You – splintered,
cracked into regrets,
sobbing "I love you, I love you,"
– too late.
Me, spluttering
choking on the taste of deadness,
all my ideals spattered
into tears upon The Skull.

We went like that –
dead men walking,

running running running!
How could we know
the missing One had come
to love all our corpses
into the land of the living?

ENOCH ARDEN

It is gilt-edged, leather worn smooth,
Tennyson duly daguerreotyped
on a title page, previously read, coddled, adored
by a Lilian Henderson I don't know, who
was kind to the children of the Infant School,
St. Mark's, South Teddington, 1884,
and left her favorite parts penned on
yellow-spotted slips slipping out.
Five pounds is a good price for this much history.

"Long lines of cliff breaking have left a chasm,"
I read, rain-spattered, wriggly-cold
and huddled tight, balled up to warm all this
Welsh green. I fly through it, lap up the
words, worry about what will happen,
(What did you write out, Alfred Lord?
What did you do to them that live,
breathe in these aged pages? Lilian!
Is it going to make me cry?)
clutch the picnic table tight
with wanting a happy ending and a thicker jacket.
I cannot go inside, cannot find a heated place –
no one must see me crying over *Enoch Arden*!

WE DO BELIEVE IN MIRACLES

(For Anya, who most exuberantly does)

Like acoustic guitars
and coconut-lime handsoap
and the back of my hand
and the nose on my face
because He said so.

Rain like thunder
soaking cracks and breaks
and potholes in July
all night till the inches build –
that's one.

You coming home and staying
after much deadness
and those lies
and that body ravaged,
tortured by the wanderlust –
that's two.

The boulder rolled
and busted from the cave
and one loving, much-forgiven
in the garden, crying
for a missing corpse –
that's why.

BEATRIX

This thirty-nine year childhood,
this dim monotony, this fog-wet life,

the large, lonely breakfast table,
the uncracked austerity of home,

the brushes flowing fantasy,
the watercolors wistful for woods –

(*Oh, my dear Noel, there were once*
four little rabbits – I know, for I was there…)

all of this together is such a small price
to pay for you,

our one wild venture,
our books in display windows,

our quivering fingers, our stuttering tongues,
your hat waving hysterically happy,

you idiotic, foolish, lovely,
face fading into the smoke, the mist,
the train rocking to the rhythm of perfection.

All of this together such a small price to pay for our
few hours of heartthrob and utopia.

NEVERTHELESS COME AUTUMN

the ocean-blue bowl won't
refuse to bruise, won't hold it back
from the gaping earth-wounds.

There will still come
water, chill wind and happy
goosebumps,

and in the utmost corners of oaks,
leaves laughing.

(First published in the *Montucky Review*)

DELIRIUM

(After *Great Expectations*)

I shall be starched and titled,
and styled a landed gent.
Marsh-squelching wood wheels take me
out in the way she went!
I shall have penitential
codfish and oysters sent
back through the rank river-grass,
the beachland, twilit dusk,
lighting the way for the cart
that comes because I must
pay you some kind of pension
for the little boy you lost.
I chased the one perfect woman,
pounded her heart of snow
packed into ice and crystal,
so many years ago.
(Not that she did not bid me leave,
but that I could not go!)
Should I someday be cornered,
famous and portly, great,
grave in the eyes of the wild
crowd, and a man of estate –
should I be led before the
populace – lined to wait –
put on a podium and
asked for the time of day,
what, before all those people,
what should I find to say?
I who had but few good things,
and threw them all away?

Not wishful to be intruding,
as how you're on the mend,
I shall be gone come morning,
coach rumbling 'round the bends,
You'll do better without me. —Joe
P.S. Ever the best of friends

FOR A BOY-CHILD

I can plant dream-seeds in the crevices,
     water them by moon-sliver light,
     soft-fingered cradle-rocking – child,
I can snap the grimy green of weeds and
     cut the choking tendrils from your heart,
     grow you up straight, sun-tilted to light.

I can give you frost-cold nights,
     a man-strong chest and wind-wild feet,
     fair-play, mercy and competition.
I can teach you the ropes – how to walk them tight
     and how to keep in boundaries and how
     some should be swiped clean, split, Gordian knots.

I can gift you with the globe –
     grasshoppers and Shakespeare and
     canvas colors and karate and
all of me can be gifted, yours
     down to the measured heaving
     of my love-heavy heart.

But about the metamorphosis –
     as to growing grey grave and gleeful,
     quiet-wording, wise-tongued and childlike –
oh, child! – only you can do that.

KATCZINSKY

"You might have spared yourself that," says an orderly.
I look at him without comprehending.
He points to Kat. "He is stone dead."
                    (Erich Maria Remarque, All Quiet on the Western Front)

Must, Paul
Must pick up his dwindled pounds
of skin spilled red and go.
We commandeered a goose,
dripped grease, closer than lovers,
minute sparks, outside night and
the circle of death.
We are two boys commandeered,
dragged into the nightmare,
brothers by our very breath.
When he is taken I will not have
one friend left.

NEVER NEVER LAND

"Love does not begin and end the way we seem to think it does.
Love is a battle, love is a war, love is a growing up."
—James A. Baldwin

He is crying because he has lost his
shadow, Wendy-lady. He is not lonely
or abandoned; he does not need you.
He does not even want you – he wants
always to be a little boy and to have fun.
Besides, he was not crying.

The loved children are unseeing, pulses
thudding in time with the knocking
of novelty, ready to up and away, and
tingling with fairy-dust, peopling
the fascinating globes of bleak fantasy
(three-mooned and no one grows up).

Love is a war where the happy thoughts
lose, transcended. And in the end,
love is a growing up. Not blind,
old Shakespeare, but farther-seeing:
2nd Star to the Right, Straight on 'til Morning,
and leaves the curtains blowing.

THE IMPORTANCE
OF BEING EARNEST

The importance of being earnest – of being
      wild-eyed and wakeful when you ask,
      of taking all your creeping death to task,
of holding to a battered hope that seeing
      is less blessed and less lovely in the mind
      of God than the foolish left behind
to hear of it in later days and, having waited
      for a sign and being given none, to take
      the Story, love it hard and for its sake
to cling, to even die – cannot be overrated.

WHEN THIS IS OVER

You will live in a house with indiscriminate quirks and lovelinesses like a drippy faucet or windy pane that lets the drafts whistle. You will set traps for the rodents and put out ant poison and water the apricot trees in spite of yourself. You will eat at buffets and tip your waiters and take cold walks in the mornings while the world is tinged with dawnlight. You will still read novels and *National Geographic* magazines and say *good morning* to your neighbors and answer the phone. After awhile, you will want to have children noisy in the backyard again and give them cookies before they leave and teach them to say *please* and *thank you*. When this is over you will be a bit stronger, cry easier, and spend more money on ice cream.

(First published in Issue 3 of Emerge Literary Journal)

SAINT CRISPIN'S DAY

(with my respects to W. Shakespeare)

I.

If we are truly marked to die,
our bodies one by one,
bleared and blood-pooled to be food
for birds of carrion,

praise be to God it is but us!
We do not need our brothers
cold here – we do not need to rob
more women of their lovers.

And if to live, we would not have
more here to share the glory –
we have met hell, come through and would
be heroes of our story.

He with no stomach for this fight
let him be on his way!
Who fears to die with us – we won't
die in his company.

II.

Upon the day when you shall strip
your sleeve and show your scars,
you shall tell of the burning, of
the blood and of the wars.

Old men forget, yet all shall be
forgot, cobwebbed in years,

and you still reel, this battle-cry
as music in your ears:

AWAKE! You gentlemen abed,
you can't see us today
but there will come a time you hang
on every word we say

about the way the arrows flew,
the plunging of the spears,
and oh! shall call yourselves accursed
because you were not here.

WAX AND ALL

You are eating apples in the airport –
apples on the corner of a stiff seat quickly
before boarding and takeoff.

We share space in a transit place
and all that is and was is here. We are
in between all the worlds there ever were, sure
of flight and light turbulence
        light turbulence.

And you are eating apples. You
are eating their perfect, unbruised
store-bought selves, wax and all.

I'll want to lord it over Napoleon,
when we strap in, ask about the elephants
when we clear alps in clear air,
swear I see his footprints, dents
        in the ice of ages –
pages of a history of walking,
dreaming, maybe talking about this,
centuries all the way back to Icharus.
And what are you doing here?

You are eating spongy apples.
You are sitting hunched on a bench
with your boots through the handle
of your duffel bag and your fingers
greedy, grabbing apples.

Da Vinci's wooden wings would

wobble, flop a little, fall right back down to
ground state, half-ashamed, inanimate
fifty hundred feet below, so
            far we wouldn't even know.
But we are going to fly today,
pay our little bit, be done with it and
board, row on row and unsurprised
take to the skies in carelessness and
            take a nap.
We are here suspended over the open
ended scheme of things, our heartbeats not fast,
last week's paper under our noses,
jaws closed, un-white knuckles not clutching,
            us here touching sky.
We are hurtling through air
 – high – where unprotected breath
is death by ice-sheets on the lungs
and engine tongues are flapping,
            mapping out a soaring way.

And you are eating apples.

ENFEEBLING

The way we are looking on dead stars,
circling the smile of the moon. The way
it was in another age this luminescence
was launched. The way that maybe the
triceratops rattled the crust of the earth,
leviathan pulsed the ocean when the
light of those stars went forth to seek out
the inky corners of the world. The way
we might be looking on blank black, really,
and wonderstruck by the light of stars
that are dust in the rings of planets.

THE SHADOW OF THE RANSOMING WOOD

                              This room that is empty
                 is crowded with heartbreak
and all their sharpie-markered pleadings
                 drip bloody
                 in the shadow of the ransoming wood.

                              "Your sins are forgiven you," He said,
                 boomed it loud, shattered windows,
and sliced up the separating veil
                              and everyone heard it
                              rip.

But in the noise of the collective gasp,
                 the choking intake of outraged breath,
                 the sob of celebration,
no one heard his lowered voice say,
                 "Get up and walk."

                 And they throng in numbers
                 to take the gift and line the altar
with their beds of paralysis
                 and weep inadequacy and never even try
                              to get up.

                 Why the bloody flesh and the sunken eyes
and the wet cheeks and the desperate gaze
                 when all your multitude of ghastly sins
                              are forgiven?

THE KNOWING TREE

Take me back to the Knowing Tree,
for I have grown haughty of heart
and I have forgotten our common fate
as wanderers in the dark.

Sit me down at its tumid base,
tucked into its gnarled roots,
swollen and tangled these ten thousand years –
give me the bitter fruit.

"You shall be lords, shall rule," He said.
"And do not eat of the tree."
And we have remembered the first command
but trampled the second, and see

we are as lords and rule and yet
stumble and babble and fail
and our tower is leaning sideways
and somehow we never prevail.

Take me back to the tree, I say –
all of the glory grows dim.
For we once partook of the Knowing Tree
and must eat it again and again.

SUPERLATIVE

Don't use words too big for the subject: don't say "infinitely" when you
mean "very"; otherwise you'll have no word left when you want to talk
about something really infinite. —C.S.Lewis

Never say savor when you only mean taste –
one is a holding on the tongue and an intoxication
and the other is cursory, a sampling, connoting
reluctance to bask. Never say a thing you don't mean.

Never say agony for pain or vast for very big or
love for the agitated chemistry of bodies unknown
to each other. If you say eternal for longevity, how
will you ever convince us of undying things?

Never say always for most of the time, or downpour
for the dribbling of hesitant rain. If you say you
believe in something you only hope tremulously to
be true, how shall we be made to understand faith?

Never say never when you only mean, *"not at any time*
in the past or the future as far as we know." Because you
might not know. And when you truly need to say,
"I will never leave you, nor forsake you," you will hear it
echoed back at you: the riotous mockery of a world
hungry for reasons to doubt. Tell us the whole truth
and nothing but the truth, so help you God.

(First published in *Quantum Poetry Magazine*)

THE JOKE *(for Jonah)*

The joke is on you if you are running,
slipshod and sliding onto the wharf,
flinging your luggage and frantic, escaping
to waves by the glimmering star of the north.

The joke is on you if you are refusing.
Am I hushed in my temple and cowering?
Shall I come to you to hear your counsel?
You who know nothing of anything?

The joke is on you and your puny fist shaking:
hear how the surf in the blackness roars,
churning around the white whale bellies?
the laughter of heaven shaking the stars?

CONFESSION
(After Job 33-42)

I too was pinched off from a piece of clay,
I too modeled by omnipotence and flanked
by things too wonderful for me: waterskins
I cannot tilt for the massing dirt and the
streaking lights that never come to me for orders.

"I had heard of you by the hearing of the ear,
but now my eye sees you"

and everything is shattered.

APOLOGETICS

We are eager to defend you, we come armed with
footnotes, poise, and crimson-inky pens
to vindicate the ways of God to men.

We are breathless in love and chivalrous, anxious
to uncover petrified horse bones,
wind patterns, life-teeming stones.

We are so sure – so very sure – and counter
every claim, dismantle every doubt, attack
with pictures and with proofs. We've got your back.

Yet it is not you who need upholding. But us, and if
we misplace our pamphlets, disorder the shelf,
you never have trouble explaining yourself.

HALLELUJAH CHORUS

"Live like you like it here."
 -Miriam Marston

Adelphoi, are you certain of unshuttered eyes?
Full cognizant, comprehending?
I think not, let me be plain:
I shall tell you the story again,
cap sudden your sorry pretending.

He came like the smell of the rain on the wind,
earth-heavy, but hinting at sky,
And we who were fixed on the fish and the hook
and never before could be bothered to look
looked up as he passed us by.

He lived like the sun on the frost-locked leaves
and loosened our beings within,
but best of all was the way He died,
for he plunked the planet on its side
and it's never been toppled again.

Adelphoi, your eyes are as wells of sleep
and the water-thin milk in your cups
has sickened my soul to its very core.
Don't you know what you draw breath for
on the globe that is right side up?

CHRISTMAS IS A HOUSE

(For G.K., who prompted the question)

where the haloed baby blows the
birthday candles every day,
and the coming faithful keep coming;
where the Herald Angels Oratorio
echoes down the ages –
and a very, very big house
because there are a lot of the Happy Few.

Christmas is a house where the
last cut the line, sit closest
to the manger, see the master first.
And the least of these – the voices all
unheard, unlistened to, dragged
from the gutter and all the
back-alleys – crowd the feast-table.

Christmas is a house in a blizzard –
right smack dab in a world all
cloaked with snow; where the screaming
wind throws the flakes in swirls against the walls,
where one candle in a window all iced over
calls the children in – the only house where
a baby crying rocks the globe from pole to pole.

THE IMAGE

He will stand one time in the bloom of the sun,
the water-beads coursing his face,
the flesh and blood rippling under his skin;
I taste it and see it — taste

the color blue in his seeing stones,
red on his tongue — and stare
at rainbows in the thousand drops
of river he sprays from his hair.

I have decided to stay and watch
every toss of his head,
looking on him and his beautifulness
and yet seeing yours instead.

Friend who has fired the kingfishers
and flamed the dragonflies —
they catch your light however they move
and beam it out of their eyes.

RESIDENCE

(After Jeremiah 29:4-7)

A word has gone out to the exiled ones:
'build houses and water the grapes.'
A ghastly phrase for the watchful eyes:
'unpack your bags,' and a high surprise:
'carve curtain-rods for your drapes.

The weaving of black and the cloth of the tears
you shall iron and steam and proceed
to fold for the hangers and file away,
for there will be no departures today,
and there are brown acres to seed.'

There has been presented a grievous command:
'root almonds and olives also.
You shall have weddings and funerals here.
It will not be this year or next year,
and some of you will not go.'

To the impatient, the shack-dwelling ones:
'nail you a barn and cut hay.
Cultivate roses and ripen the sand,
grow you a lovely affair with the land,
because you are going to stay.'

...and day by day this pathway smooths
since first I learned to love it...

(Pauline T.)

www.ingramcontent.com/pod-product-compliance
Lightning Source LLC
Chambersburg PA
CBHW031527040426
42445CB00009B/428